Ideas for Quick and Easy

Easy

Keto Dinners

SARAH JORDAN

TABLE OF CONTENTS

INTRODUCTION

Hey dear friend!

If you are reading this book, you are most likely tired of constant fight with the overweight, break-downs with cheat meals and complicated diets which deprive you of all gastronomic pleasures and make you starve.

There is a huge variety of diets and "proper" methods of healthy eating, which sometimes contradict each other. Not all of them will help you to be slim93, healthy, and full of energy.

I've experienced it myself. Please keep in mind that I'm not one of super-girls who have lost 200 pounds in 6 months and changed their lives in 365 degrees. My story is more about exploring the ways to live a healthy lifestyle, being concentrated, mindful, effective, stay in a good mood, and have enough time for my family and business.

I have never had any big issues with overweight – thanks to my mom's and dad's genetical heritage. My mom is 65 now, and she weighs about 99 pounds, can you believe it? She can eat whatever she wants and never gains lousy pounds.

I'm not that lucky haha, although I'm a little slim, during my life, my weight was moving between 103 and 115 pounds – depending on how long my holidays were at the all-inclusive, all-you-can-eat resort. Fortunately, I managed to lose weight quickly after two pregnancies (my boys are 5 and 14 now). However, the last few pounds were still there, although I tried hard to get rid of them.

I was worried about other issues – how can I be productive with my business, team, and have free time for the family? I launched my travel agency 2 years ago and have to invest lots of time and energy in it. Also, I'm a wife and a mother of 2 guys who need attention; you know what I mean!

I have tried a bunch of different diets – Atkins, low-fat, raw vegan and practiced a vegetarian lifestyle for about 4 years. Atkins was more or less OK, but I didn't feel well while practicing it – I constantly was sleepy, didn't have strength at all, and a couple of months the problems with the kidneys and the periods showed up.

I spent a few months on traditional nutrition with counting calories. A well-functioning weight loss system, but with one disadvantage: maintaining a stable weight was impossible. At least I failed. Once I skipped a couple of workouts or ate a couple of extra ounces - in the morning plus 1 kg. Moreover, when I ate too little (800–1000 kcal), the weight did not leave quickly either, but I suffered from horrible mood swings – from pure happiness to depression.

The whole experience with vegetarian and low-fat diets didn't make the results I needed. A few extra pounds were still there, I had flare-ups and eczema spots, had hunger hits regularly (hAngry), felt guilty after having a cheat-meal, blamed myself for the lack of willpower. Mood-swings have been driving me crazy – especially emotional splashes while communicating with my boys. Screaming and yelling mom – this is not what they want, right?

The other big problem was the lack of brain power, focus, and mental clarity. For me, it was a challenge to quit a stable office position with a good salary and start my own business. I was very inspired by this opportunity! Can you imagine how many things you have to do to make a new agency work? Since then, I realized that I could not make the desired results due to my physical issues. What a shame! I often remember myself lying on the sofa and surfing through Facebook instead of getting things done or cooking dinner for my family. Especially after having a piece of "healthy" whole-grain bread or an unsweetened dessert made of dried fruits. I was losing time and money!

I was trying to find out how effectivity was connected to eating habits. I figured out that high-carb food kicks me out of the working process and makes me lazy, sluggish, and dull like crap. My work stopped after having a "healthy" low-fat granola with sweet fruits and dried raisins. Really? Unbelievable!

When my family doctor mentioned about Ketogenic diet, and I started exploring it – I literally could not sleep for a week. I read about 7000 pages in 1 week and was so inspired! Eating fat and losing weight – what could be more shocking and amazing? Eggs, bacon, oils – all the products I was deprived of such a long time are now allowed! I was also surprised by how simple this diet is. Most of the foods are known from childhood and can be easily found at any grocery store.

I decided to try right now. First, I picked out a shelf in the fridge only for my keto-challenge and removed all forbidden products to other places. Then I made a shopping list and went to the grocery store. Was not hard to find all ingredients in one place. Though some of them (like psyllium or avocado oil), I ordered online.

Every time I went shopping (once a week), I planned what I'm going to cook during the week and took the list of necessary foods with me to a grocery store. It helped me to avoid buying some high-carb snack impulsively.

The first thing that surprised me – I stopped feeling hunger at all! Was it me? Really? Usually, I had breakfast around 8 am, and after 11 o'clock, I experienced a wild hunger and began searching for some snacks. After starting my keto experience, I realized that I don't even think about the food at least till 1 pm! Unbelievable. Moreover, I didn't have to eat an elephant in the morning to feel satisfied until lunch.

When the body switches from gaining energy from carbohydrates to fats, keto flu can happen. However, I was lucky to avoid it because I drank lots of water with salt and used magnesium from time to time. It is the key to good feeling during the adaptation period; please keep it in mind.

I didn't expect the success to happen so quickly. 4 kg suddenly left me instantly in the first 3 weeks. I could not believe the scales in the morning! After all, I was full; I ate butter and cheese for dinner, how could it be minus 0,5 kg per night? Magic? No, just keto!

Later, I noted the positive effect of keto on the skin condition. I got rid of acne and eczema spots, my skin became smooth like silk. I don't even need to apply the cream. No more migraines, constipation, lack of power, and inflammations! Moreover, I didn't feel any pain during my period.

The taste became sharper. I began to feel previously unknown tastes of ordinary food. The scent has become much clearer, and notices smells that had not been noticed before.

The most important and valuable result was emotional stability, a constant feeling of satiety and health, great focus, concentration, and absolute mind clarity. I managed to do 3 times more things during the day than before! Incredible! I noticed the results in the business immediately – of course, in US dollars. I gained lots of free time for my family, and my effectiveness became 3 times bigger!

If I break and overeat something, then this is the same keto-food. I can overdo with nuts and cheese because I love them so much. It does not kick me out of ketosis and does not affect the weight. For the first time in my life, I think I found a comfortable diet for myself. That's why I decided to write a book about my keto-experience and share my quick delicious recipes with you. No sophisticated medical terms, complicated recipes which take 2 hours to cook, or rare ingredients available only in special stores. I want you to remember – KETO IS EASY.

I hope you fall in love with the keto diet and make it a new stage of your life. You change the eating habits, improve your health, and get rid of overweight. Moreover, gain a strong focus, concentration, and high effectivity as a pleasant bonus! Once you join our Ketoholic community, you never regret it!

WHAT IS KETO DIET ABOUT?

- Keto is not only about the numbers on a scale, ounces in a plate or switching from sugar to stevia. It is abo24ut feeling good and achieving higher results in your life.

- Keto is about the comforting weight without starving, self-violence and deprivation of all gastronomic pleasures which are important for us from childhood. We are used to having food as a reward, gift, celebration! So why do we have to refuse?

- Keto diet is about the whole, healthy products without sugar, gluten, and other toxic ingredients. High-quality food charges you with pure energy and keeps your body slim and attractive. Once you see the result, you will not agree to have another kind of lifestyle.

- Keto food is TASTY. You probably know that some diets limit eating salt, spices, and fat. But not keto! Same with sweets – instead of sugar you use natural sweeteners which make every dessert delicious and guilt-free.

- Keto is about stable hormones and macros in the blood. It normalizes the satiety hormone leptin and the hormone of sexual desire testosterone. You feel free of constant hunger. Emotional and psychical state stabilizes, no more mood swings and break-downs. Forget about being "angry because hungry" (hangry).

- Ketones create the long-lasting source of pure energy that releases you from constantly thinking about the food and counting minutes till the next meal. You don't have to prepare food containers or snacks to take with you to the office or a restaurant – keto food options are available at most eateries.

- On keto, you see the physical health improvements. When you start eating whole products, you easily forget about toxic foods like sugar, wheat flour, and processed crap. You already know what happens to your body when you feed it with junk foods and you don't want it anymore?

- You better your cognitive performance. You will be surprised how focused, concentrated, and mindful you become on keto! You manage to do much more things per hour than before. Moreover, don't waste time surfing through the internet or lying on the sofa for hours after a heavy meal. The mind becomes clear, like an x-ray.

- Everything is clearer, brighter, faster on keto. The brain is clean and effective because of excluding ingredients which cause inflammation – sugar, gluten, processed food.

- Keto is a comfortable way to lose weight. When you switch from getting energy from the carbs to ketone power, you start burning your fat when the energy from the food is over. You maintain the comfort calories deficit, which is not dangerous but very effective for the body.

- Keto maintains the long-lasting effect. It is not a diet or an emergency action to fit the wedding dress. Keto is a lifestyle. It considers the mindful and attentive way of planning your meal program, self-care, self-respect, and efficient sleeping.

EASY STEPS TO START THE KETOGENIC LIFESTYLE

- Plan your meal program and follow it accurately. It helps to maintain new eating habits and prevent impulsive spending money on some unexpected stuff.

- First 3-4 weeks I recommend eating only home-made food to be concentrated on the quality of ingredients. It makes you sure that the food does not contain sugar, wheat flour, or gluten. You know exactly how you made a sauce or pancakes, right?

- Each meal should contain healthy fats and proteins. Avoiding high-carb foods is essential. Do not limit green veggies consumption – you cannot eat too much cilantro or green salad!

- Step by step try to switch into 3-times meals without snacking. The last meals should be taken no later than 6 pm. Feel what the body needs if you are not hungry – not necessary to eat.

- Pay attention to the quality and quantity of sleep. It is important because the satiety hormone leptin is strongly connected with the hormone of sleep – melatonin. In other words – the less you sleep, the more extra calories you eat compulsively. Try to fall asleep before 11 pm and sleep 7-8 hours.

- Read the nutrition labels carefully. Some products can contain hidden carbs or gluten (sometimes in absolutely unexpected places).

- Be rather flexible and consecutive than fanatically stubborn. Don't blame yourself for an occasional slice of pizza or piece of cake eaten at the party. The more you follow the ketogenic lifestyle, the more aware you are about the food you choose. Step by step, you will lose interest in high-carb products and will enjoy being at the party or a wedding dinner without a risk to eat something forbidden. However, if you occasionally cheated – no problem. Just notice it without blaming yourself and come back to your keto diet plan.

- Start recording everything you eat during the day into the food diary (including pieces you taste while preparing food). Fix your feelings, sensations in the body, and mood state. You will discover a lot about yourself and will notice the connection between the mood and the appetite swings. There is a wide variety of food diaries on the market, choose the best for you.

- If you feel that you are about to cheat and cannot control it, drink a glass of water and wait for 10 minutes. Alternatively, go outside and walk a few blocks. If it does not help – do 30 squats and 10 push-ups. It will reduce hunger and improve your mood. This is extremely helpful if you tend to use food as a stress relief.

- Prepare fat bombs in advance and keep them in the fridge just in case you desire to eat something sweet asap. Grocery stores and online-shops also have a wide range variety of low-carb desserts.

- Set attainable and achievable goals for keto. Do not say: "I want to be slim in one month." Plan to lose 4-5 pounds a month. You had been gaining all these extra pounds for many years, so why expect them to leave in 2 weeks? Losing weight and getting into healthy keto lifestyle is a long-distance marathon, be patient.

- Split the big goal into small stages. Set 3 kinds of targets:

    1. Short-distance goals. Something you can do right now. For example, get rid of unhealthy products or buy a membership card in the gym.
    2. Middle-distance (weekly) goals. The number of squats per minute, for example.
    3. Long-distance (1, 3, 6 months) – the number on the scale or the waist volume.

- Imagine your ideal body. How does it look like? How do you feel when you are slim, fit, and full of energy? What do other people see when they meet you? How does the whole life look like when you reached your goal? How will it affect your job, family, career? What new possibilities are available for you when you have a dream body.

- Do not blame anyone for your overweight. Who is responsible for the extra pounds you have gained? Your parents who were feeding you with sweets from childhood? Alternatively, the food manufacturers who made processed junk products? Alternatively, maybe bad genetics? No way. Stop complaining and blaming circumstances. Take responsibility for your health, life, and future. No matter what happened in the past, the future is in your hands. Start acting now!

- Drink about 2 liters of water per day. Choose reverse osmosis and add lemon – it is the natural alkalite. Take the water before meals, but never – after. Wait 50-60 minutes after a meal and then drink water. Keep a glass of water near your bed in case hunger hits you in the middle of the night.

- Find someone who will get into keto lifestyle with you. It can be just one person, a group of people, or a large community. Support groups and buddies are proven to boost the results and prevent from cheating.

- Start the workout routine. You can do yoga, running, gym, pilates, dancing, cycling – whatever makcs you happy! One small lifehack – doing sports with your friends double the results. Create a supportive WhatsApp chat where you can share pictures and motivate each other to do sports.

- If you tend to reward yourself with the food, create a new rewarding system (not connected to eating). It can be anything – a new book, beautiful lingerie, a ticket to a cinema – whatever makes you happy! It can be helpful as long as you need an external motivation.

- Weigh yourself once a week at the same time. Keep in mind that if you exercise a lot, the weight can stay at the same level, but the volumes can decrease. Muscles are quite heavy, so do not misplace them with extra pounds.

- Never go shopping when you are hungry. Otherwise, there is a risk to buy unhealthy food compulsively. Limit consumption of soda water, coffee, and alcohol –

these drinks slow down the weight loss. Keep at home lots of crunchy veggies like cucumbers and radishes – they are tasty and filling.

- Intend to lose weight and gain a slim healthy body for yourself. Not for the husband, friends, Instagram profile, or to please parents. Remember – your future is in your hands, so start creating it now. Stop comparing yourself with other people, focus on yourself instead. You are unique, enjoy it!

- Always eat at the table and never – in front of the TV or the laptop. It makes you eat more and more! Chew every piece at least 20 times and try to savor each morsel. Keto food is amazing, enjoy every piece.

- Before you go out, check the restaurants for keto options. Check the menus online or call them and make sure they have food suitable for your lifestyle.

- When you begin the keto lifestyle, limit the carb intake to the suggested rate of 20 gram a day at least the first 3 weeks. After that, your appetite will decrease significantly.

HOW TO SAVE TIME WHILE COOKING?

- Once you are ready to start the ketogenic lifestyle and become a true Ketoholic, read these simple tips about shopping and preparing food. They make your life easier and save lots of time! Although all recipes in this cookbook are easy and take about 30-35 min to prepare, they require a little patience and attention.

- Use leftovers. Keeping half of the dinner for breakfast can save plenty of time! You can put meat cubes in the salad, greens or tomatoes – in the omelet, make a sauce of parsley or dill even if they are already dry.

- Chop and freeze in advance. Imagine you bought a big piece of meat, and each time before cooking you have to thaw it for a long time. However, if you cut it into small pieces before freezing, then it will be much easier to thaw or even immediately place it into the pan. Same with vegetables! Wash, cut into pieces for frying, put in the refrigerator. Then take it out and put it in the pan.

- Plan your shopping. Before you go shopping, create a list of what you are going to buy and cook of it. Later, when you open the door of the fridge, you don't spend time for hesitating what to make for breakfast or dinner.

- When you slice or mince something, place a small garbage bin next to you (like a plastic container or a can). While cooking, put the garbage there and when you're done, throw away the waste in a large bin and wash the tank. You save time on walking to the bin. You also have to clean a smaller area.

- On weekends or when you have free time, prepare the basis for some foods. For example, boil eggs and other vegetables, chop fresh veggies: parsley, onion, pepper, lettuce, cabbage, etc. (greens can be stored in the refrigerator for several days). Having on hand all these ingredients, you can quickly cook a salad, soup, make a side dish for meat or chicken.

- Grab & Go. Prepare snacks in advance and put them in small plastic bags. In the morning you grab the bag and go to the office.

- Position furniture, appliances, and kitchen tools correctly. It saves time on moving and cleaning. Proper location includes the following:
1. The minimum distance along the triangle between the oven, sink, and refrigerator;
2. Place dishes near the sink and dishwasher;

3. Place the pots and pans between the sink and oven.

- Clean while cooking. The pieces of food will not dry on the walls, skillets, and pans, and you can remove them quickly. Moreover, after having a meal, you don't have to waste time washing a bunch of dirty dishes.

- Study the cutting and chopping techniques. Most of these routine tasks can be done quicker than you're used to. You can find many videos about it on Youtube.

- Once you have bought greens, wash them immediately, dry with a paper towel and put them in hermetic containers. Close tightly and store in the fridge on the lower shelves for up to one week. Once the dirty work is done, you don't need to wash everything individually in small portions.

- Preheat the oven in advance. When you start cooking, immediately turn on the oven or grill to warm up, or put water to boil. All ovens are different. It can take from 10 to 15 minutes. Though an electric oven with convection usually does not require pre-heating. Turn on the oven before you prepare the ingredients.

- Organize the cooking process competently. Make sure that all the ingredients are at your fingertips. The food can be easily spoiled if you spend time searching for sesame oil, while the food in the skillet starts burning in a few seconds.

- Read the whole recipe first. Before you start cooking, you should carefully study all the instructions. Then spend a few minutes to collect the ingredients, dishes, and tools. This is especially helpful when a dish requires something that you don't use every day. For example, a mixer, lemon zest remover, or a blender. It will save lots of time and help you to avoid mistakes. Pay attention to the prep and cook time. I settled an approximate time; it can vary due to the brands of ingredients and your cooking speed.

- Chop into smaller pieces. The smaller the ingredients, the faster they are cooked. Slices, diced or grated food saves lots of time. Time for cutting and chopping is included in the recipe timing.

- Bake in the middle of the oven. It allows the heat circulates evenly, so the dish does not burn. Thaw and soften ingredients in advance. Softened and warmed goods make better results.

- Make sure you put enough oil for cooking and grease the dish generously. The lack of oils can make the food burn and stuck in a pan or skillet; you will lose lots of time to remove it and clean.

- Cook extra portions and store them in the containers in the fridge. Then you have to reheat them and enjoy! Most of the keto dishes are even tastier the next day.

HOW TO USE THE RECIPES

- Most of the goods are accessible and can be found at any supermarket or grocery store. If you have any difficulties – don't hesitate to ask the grocery store personnel.

- This cookbook contains 60 easy dinner recipes which take no longer than 40 minutes to prepare. Each recipe is followed by prep time, cook time, the number of servings, and nutrition facts PER SERVING. This info helps to follow your keto plan. The nutritional information was calculated with Verywellfit.

- Before cooking, read the whole recipe first. It will help you to organize the process and not to lose time.

-

NECESSARY KITCHEN TOOLS

Whisk.

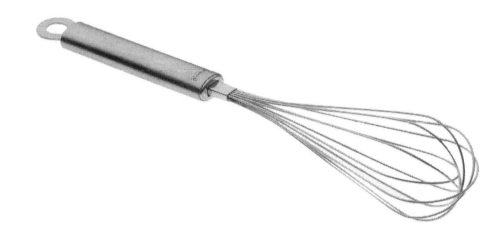

You can use it both for bulk and liquid ingredients. It helps whisk eggs or in preparing spice mixture. Better use a whisk with silicone cover – it prevents dishes from scratches.

Vegetable peeler.

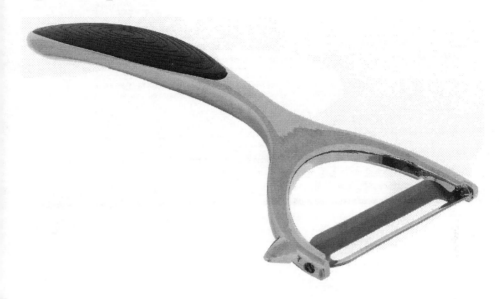

Use it instead of a usual knife. The special blade helps you to peel the vegetables and fruits quickly, evenly and safely. A peeler can look like a simple knife or might be Y-shaped with a blade located perpendicular to the handle. The first option is suitable for small round vegetables, the second - for oblong (carrots, cucumbers, sweet potatoes, oval potato varieties). There are also peelers which make the wavy shape of slices – good for food decoration.

Meat chopper.

Meat choppers can be wooden or metal and usually have a serrated surface on both sides of the head - small teeth for tender meat, large ones for rough. Metal choppers are more long-lasting, but wooden ones don't destroy meat fibers. Wooden choppers used for raw meat need to be changed as often as possible because of bacteria which accumulates inside the tree

Measure cups.

Accurate measuring ingredients is essential on keto. The result can be disappointing if you don't follow the proper proportions. The shape and material are not important; the main thing that measures should be familiar to you. The same container should contain different scales - for liquid and for bulk ingredients, which have different density and different weights for the same volume.

Kitchen Tongs.

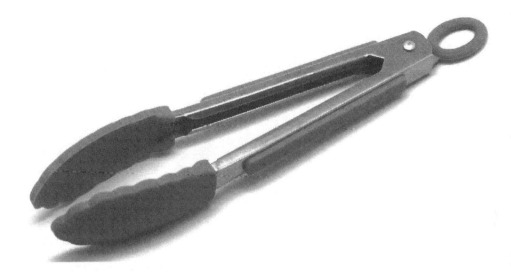

Tongs are a multifunctional and incredibly convenient accessory for the kitchen. Using tongs, you can mix greens and vegetables in a salad, transfer a steak from a skillet to a plate, turn the meat in a frying pan. In order not to damage the skin of your hands, you can also use forceps to remove food from the freezer.

Grater.

You can grate lemon zest, zucchini, cheese, etc. The more verges this accessory has, the wider is the choice of cutting thickness. The most popular ones are four-sided graters, but now you can also find hexagonal models with which you can grate cheese, vegetables, fruits, nuts, chocolate, and much more. There are also options with removable containers, meat grinder graters, multi-graders with removable nozzles, turning food into a puree and many other options - both electric and manual.

Spoons.

There are spoons which help with cooking and serving dishes. A ladle is useful if you are cooking soups and sauces – it helps to fill the plate with liquid. Skimmer (a spoon with holes) is needed to remove the foam, get the foods from the boiling water if you have pans with a non-stick coating that is easily scratched, better use a wooden or nylon skimmer.

Shoulder blades.

Flat wide shoulder blades help to turn the food in the pan or transfer the dish to a plate. Silicone scrapers of various sizes and shapes are helpful to remove the remaining dough or other creamy mixtures from the walls of the mixing bowl. The shoulder blades are not only silicone but also metal, plastic, wooden. Better to have several types of them from different materials for different surfaces and purposes.

Sieve.

It can be used for a wide range of kitchen needs. You can use it to drain washed veggies or rinse canned beans, remove large-leaved spices from sauces, get blanched vegetables from boiling water, sift dry ingredients and even make citrus juice. If you only need a sieve for sifting loose ingredients, an excellent choice is a mug-shaped one with a special pen, pressing on which activates the sifting mechanism. For hot foods choose sieve made of metal or heat-resistant plastic.

Cutting board.

The importance of this item in the kitchen is invaluable. The board protects the working surface from damage by a knife and makes cutting and chopping products more convenient. Boards can be made of wood, glass, plastic, and some modern models are made of flexible silicone (you can even mix the dough on them). Your personal preferences may determine the choice of material, and the number of boards in the kitchen should correspond to the number of types of products you cut (a separate board for meat, fish, vegetables and fruits, bread.

Pan/skillet.

Look for skillets and pans with a thick and heavy base. The thicker the pan, the more evenly it will conduct heat. It will also keep warm better. Aluminum, stainless steel, and copper are ideal materials for dishes. When choosing, focus on quality but not quantity.

Silicone brush.

This brush is very convenient for greasing a baking sheet or pan. This brush saves the oil from spraying it in all directions. Silicone brush can withstand temperatures from 60 to 280 degrees.

Knives.

The best knives are forged. Such models are reliable and long-lasting. When buying knives, you need to focus on quality, not quantity. A knife should feel convenient for the hand. Its weight should be evenly distributed from the handle to the tip. The blade is super important as well. A quality blade should be free of cracks, chips, stains, and streaks. The surface should be smooth, shiny, perfectly polished.

Bowls.

Essential for mixing different ingredients. You must have at least three different sizes. When buying bowls, choose the ones with high edges. The durability and cost of this item depends on the material.

Baking dish.

Useful for cooking lasagna, casserole, meat, chicken. Such dishes should look aesthetic and beautiful (in the case, the cooked dish can be put to the table).

Baking sheet.

When purchasing a baking sheet, pay attention to several parameters. It should not be too light and too thin. It should have sides: it protects the oven from unnecessary pollution. Better opt for the lighter color. In this case the baking sheet heats up slower, which protects the food from burning.

Kitchen Scales.

Can be electronic or mechanical. I suggest you choose an electronic one as they are more accurate, and also often have additional functionality. For example, in many electronic scales weight, memorization and sequential weighing of ingredients are available. Some models can calculate the volume of fluid to be weighed. Information about the weight of products and other data (if any) are displayed in electronic scales on display. Electronic scales need to work in the power supply. Most electronic kitchen scales are powered by AA or AAA batteries. Some models use the so-called 'tablet' batteries.

Timer.

Free your head from worrying about the timing. There are mechanical and electronic options. A mechanical one is more expensive and long-lasting because it does not suffer from the humidity in the kitchen. Electronic timer is cheaper and works from the batteries.

Immersion blender.

The more powerful the blender, the faster it works, the fewer chances it has to overheat, and the more solid products it can process. If you want to chop ice or to process complex products (meat or chicken, for example), a 600-800 W device will suit you well. 5-8 speeds will be enough. For the simple tasks, a blender with two speeds is also suitable. When choosing a blender, opt for the one with metal nozzles so you can blend even a boiling soup.

Waffle maker.

When choosing a waffle iron, please pay attention to its surface coating. It can be made of Teflon or ceramics. Ceramic coating has long durability and environmental cleanliness but can be scratched with sharp tools (metal blades, knives). Teflon cover minimizes the risk of burning and allows you to cook waffles without using oil, but over time, the Teflon may wear off. Waffle makers with interchangeable plates allowing to cook waffles of various shapes. The optimal power for a home waffle maker is 700-800 W.

Food processor.

A multifunctional device which makes cooking easier and saves plenty of time! Your best friend in the kitchen. There are 2 types of food processors:

Food processor – blender. Food processor – "blender." Actually, it is an upgraded model of the mixer, quite simple and affordable. It has a base of a motor inside and buttons outside. Might include a chopper bowl, mixing container, citrus press and cutting discs. Go for this kind of food processor if your dishes require much cutting and grinding.

Food processor – "sewing machine." This device is more expensive and heavier but more professional. Such food processors are usually equipped with a full-fledged juicer or meat grinder, has a wide range variety of mixing paddles. Go for it if you intend to make lots of creams or soups.

Foil.

Can be found at any grocery store or online shop. The important parameter is thickness. The foil can be two types - 9 microns and 14. The first option is good for storing cooked products, and the second - for baking as it is more heat-resistant.

Oven.

For cooking, keto choose an electric oven 60 or 90 cm wide
with a grill, convection, spit and telescopic rails. Choose an
oven with child protection function and 3-4 glasses if you
have a small child. The advantages of an electric oven are: an
option to set the exact temperature, uniform warming up,
automatic programs, and the ability of simultaneous baking
on two levels. The disadvantages – it warms up slower than
a gas oven and requires more energy.

A gas oven can also work. It is more simple and durable, but there are some disadvantages: small temperature range, impossible to set the exact temperature, food can be baked unevenly, no automatic programs.

Other kitchen tools.

Forks

Teaspoons

Tablespoons

Plates

EASY KETO DINNERS
POULTRY

Georgian Style Chicken

Prep time 10 min
Cook time 20 min

Yield 2 servings

Fat 14,4
Protein 33,3
Carbs 1,5
Fiber 0,4
Calories 270

Ingredients

2 chicken thighs
2 garlic cloves
½ teaspoon oregano
½ teaspoon paprika
Himalayan rock salt to taste
3 tablespoons ghee butter

Instructions

- Smash garlic cloves with pressure and mix with spices in a small bowl
- Hit chicken thighs until they are soft
- Brush the chicken with a mixture of garlic and spices on each side
- Heat the ghee butter in the skillet
- Put the chicken inside and press with something heavy
- Fry for 10 minutes each side or until cooked
- Serve with a green salad

Chicken & Cheesy Mushrooms

Prep time 5 min
Cook time 33 min

Yield 2 servings

Fat 19,9
Protein 23,6
Carbs 4
Fiber 1
Calories 282

Ingredients

6 champignons
100 gr minced chicken meat
1 teaspoon coconut oil
50 gr creamy cheese
Himalayan rock salt to taste
Spices to taste
Ghee butter for frying
3 teaspoons grated parmesan

Instructions

- Preheat the oven too 400F
- Remove stipes from mushroom caps and chop them (mushroom caps set aside)
- Mix chopped mushroom stipes with minced chicken meat
- Melt ghee butter in a skillet over medium-high heat
- Fry mushrooms with minced meat in the skillet for about 10 min
- Cool down a bit and mix with cream cheese
- Fill mushroom caps with this mix
- Place in the baking dish, add coconut oil and put in the oven for 20 minutes
- Sprinkle the grated parmesan on the top and let it melt

Juicy Chicken Wings

Prep time 5 min
Cook time 27 min

Ingredients

1 ½ pounds chicken wings
½ teaspoons black pepper
½ teaspoon dried peppermint
½ teaspoon Himalayan pink salt
2 tablespoons coconut oil
½ teaspoon dried thyme
½ teaspoon red pepper
Stevia to taste

Yield 4 servings

Fat 19,5
Protein 49,4
Carbs 1,4
Fiber 0,3
Calories 388

Instructions

- Preheat the oven to 400F
- Mix all spices with stevia and coconut oil and sprinkle mixture over chicken evenly
- Put on a wire rack over a cookie sheet and bake 25 minutes, or until the chicken is soft
- Serve with a green salad.

Keto Chicken Curry

Prep time 8 min
Cook time 15 min

Yield 2 servings

Fat 23,7
Protein 29,1
Carbs 1,5
Fiber 0,3
Calories 326

Ingredients

2 servings pre-roasted chicken thighs with skin
1 cup full-fat coconut milk
½ teaspoon yellow curry powder
1 tablespoon ghee butter
½ teaspoon cayenne pepper
1 teaspoon Himalayan rock salt
Black pepper to taste

Instructions

- Warm up the chicken in the oven for 5 minutes
- Cut into ½ inch pieces
- Melt ghee butter in a skillet over medium-high heat
- Mix coconut milk with spices and put into skillet
- Please bring it to a boil, stirring constantly
- When it starts boiling remove from the heat and let it rest for 1 minute
- Place in a bowl and add chicken, toss well
- Serve with lettuce or other green salad

Chicken rolls

Prep time 8 min
Cook time 15 min

Yield 2 servings

Fat 63,8
Protein 74,6
Carbs 22
Fiber 8,5
Calories 830

Ingredients

250 g cream cheese
1 soft avocado
1 tablespoon keto mayo
¼ teaspoon dried garlic
450 g prebaked chicken
2 tablespoons lemon juice
1 fresh green pepper
2 cucumbers

Instructions

- Remove cream cheese out of the fridge and let in warm up a bit
- Place in a blender and whip for 2 minutes
- Smash avocado with a fork (remove the skin first), add lemon juice and mix well
- Add salt to taste
- Cut cucumbers and green pepper in straws
- Mix whipped cheese, avocado, keto mayo, garlic seasoning and blend for about 1 minute until it looks like a heavy spread
- Slice the chicken and brush it with the heavy cream, place a few straws of cucumber and pepper on the top
- Make rolls of it

Chicken & Veggie Stew

Prep time 7 min
Cook time 30 min

Ingredients

400 gr chicken thighs (no skin and bones)
1 big zucchini
2 eggplants
1 fresh green bell pepper
1 tablespoon keto mayo
Himalaya rock salt to taste
Spices to taste
2 tablespoons ghee butter

Yield 2 servings

Fat 32,4
Protein 26,9
Carbs 26
Fiber 21,9
Calories 537

Instructions

- Cut the chicken in small pieces
- Add mayo, salt and spices to taste
- Mix well and set aside
- Remove the skin from zucchini and eggplants, cut in cubes
- Cut the bell pepper in small cubes also
- Preheat ghee butter in the skillet, place the chicken inside and fry for 10 minutes over high heat
- Add vegetables, salt to taste and stew for 15 minutes or until cooked

Chicken & Celery Salad

Prep time 5 min
Cook time 20 min

Ingredients

200 gr chicken fillet
3 tablespoons olive oil
2 tablespoons raw vinegar
2 celery stalks
2 tablespoons lemon juice
2 cups fresh spinach
1 cup chopped fresh parsley
Salt and pepper to taste

Yield 2 servings

Fat 12
Protein 11,6
Carbs 2
Fiber 1
Calories 161

Instructions

- Cut the chicken into medium thick slices, brush with salt and pepper
- Heat the oil in the skillet and cook the chicken for 10-13 minutes
- Remove from the heat, season with vinegar and cover the bowl
- Meanwhile, chop the spinach and cut the celery, season with salt, pepper and lemon juice
- Garnish the chicken with the salad

Chicken Greek Style

Prep time 15 min
Cook time 20 min

Ingredients

400 gr chicken breast, uncooked
½ red onion
2 cups chopped dill
2 tablespoons olive oil
4 tablespoons lemon juice
8 cherry tomatoes
100 gr rocket salad
1 cucumber
Salt and pepper to taste

Yield 4 servings

Fat 11,3
Protein 24,9
Carbs 24
Fiber 7,1
Calories 303

Instructions

- Dice the onion into thin rings, place in a small bowl and mix with 2 tablespoons of lemon juice and salt. Let it rest for 10 minutes, stir a couple of times
- Slice the chicken breasts in halves, brush with salt and pepper all sides
- Heat the large skillet with the oil, place the chicken inside
- Fry 10 minutes per side
- Meanwhile, slice the cucumber, cherry tomatoes in halves, mince the dill and the rocket
- When the chicken is ready to transfer it to a plate
- Garnish with minced greens, tomatoes, cucumber and onion marinade
- Serve hot

Turkey Spring Rolls

Prep time 15 min
Cook time 5 min

Ingredients

450 gr grilled turkey (pre-cooked or store-bought – check the labels!)
1 cup cream cheese (softened)
1 tablespoon keto mayo
1 tablespoon lemon juice
1 green bell pepper
2 fresh cucumbers
1 avocado
½ teaspoon garlic powder
1 fresh stalk dill

Yield 3 servings

Fat 44,8
Protein 24,4
Carbs 36
Fiber 11,5
Calories 650

Instructions

- Whip softened cream cheese in a bowl until creamy
- Slice avocado in halves, remove the pulp and smash it with a fork, add lemon juice, salt and mix well
- Slice the cucumbers and bell pepper in thin straws
- Add the avocado pulp, mayo and garlic powder to the whipped cheese
- Whisk with the mixer for 1 minute till the sauce thickens
- Slice the turkey into thin slices. Put a layer of avocado and cheese sauce on every slice, put a few cucumber and pepper straws and a small stalk of parsley
- Make rolls

66

Mozzarella & Chicken Casserole

Prep time 8 min
Cook time 20 min

Yield 5 servings

Fat 16,9
Protein 25,5
Carbs 3,3
Fiber 0,6
Calories 271

Ingredients

1 grilled chicken (home-made or store-bought)
200 gr cherry tomatoes
1 cup mozzarella cheese
3 tablespoons pesto sauce
1 cup heavy cream
½ cup grated Parmesan cheese
Salt and pepper to taste
2 tablespoons fresh chopped parsley
1 tablespoon chopped cilantro

Instructions

- Preheat the oven to 420F
- Chop the chicken into small cubes
- Cut the tomatoes in halves, shred the mozzarella cheese
- Mix in a bowl with the chicken
- Add pesto sauce, half grated parmesan cheese, season with salt and pepper
- Place in a baking dish and put in the oven
- Cook for 20 minutes until golden crispy
- Top with chopped greens

Chicken Fillet with Asparagus and Parmesan

Prep time 5 min
Cook time 25 min

Yield 3 servings

Fat 23,1
Protein 16,7
Carbs 6,6
Fiber 2,1
Calories 293

Ingredients

3 chicken fillets, no skin
12 asparagus spears
½ cup creamy cheese
½ teaspoon cumin powder
1 tablespoon ghee butter
1 cup grated parmesan
Salt and pepper to taste
1 tablespoon coconut oil

Instructions

- Preheat the oven to 380F
- Cut the chicken fillet and open it (it should look like a book)
- Brush the chicken with salt, pepper and cumin powder
- Split the cheese into 3 parts and spread it at one half of each chicken fillet
- Put the asparagus and "close" the book, fix it with a toothpick
- Heat the oil in the skillet over medium heat and fry the chicken for 5-6 minutes per side
- Remove to the baking form and sprinkle with grated parmesan
- Bake for 5 minutes until the cheese is crispy

VEGGIES

Keto Pasta Carbonara

Prep time 5 min
Cook time 15 min

Servings 2

Fat 40,7
Protein 32,2
Carbs 16,2
Fiber 4,3
Calories 561

Ingredients

2 cups of riced cauliflower
8 slices uncooked bacon
3 tablespoons heavy cream
1 tablespoon oregano
1 teaspoon paprika
6 minced garlic cloves
Red pepper to taste
Himalayan rock salt to taste

Instructions

- Preheat a large skillet on medium heat.
- Cut bacon into ½ inch pieces with a sharp knife
- Cook the bacon in the skillet for 6-7 minutes, stirring permanently until the bacon is crispy
- Add the minced garlic, stir well, cook until browned
- Add in the cauliflower, salt and spices, heavy cream
- Stir until thickened and creamy. Serve hot.

Green Keto Waffles

Prep time 8 min
Cook time 25 min

Ingredients

2 eggs
1 tablespoon cream
50 gr ghee butter
25 gr coconut flour
1 spoon baking powder
Salt and pepper to taste
1 cup chopped greens – spinach, spring onion, rosemary, etc

Servings 4 pieces

Fat 15,7
Protein 4
Carbs 6,3
Fiber 3,5
Calories 180

Instructions

- Preheat, the waffle maker
- Separate egg whites, put them in blender and whip until foamy
- In other cup mix egg yolks, cream, melted ghee butter, and chopped greens
- Add coconut flour, baking powder, salt, and pepper and mix well
- Stir in egg whites slowly and carefully to save air bubbles inside (dough should be thick like heavy cream)
- Grease the waffle maker and put the dough inside
- Fry till crispy
- Serve with heavy cream

Cheesy Broccoli Casserole

Prep time 7 min
Cook time 30 min

Ingredients

200 gr broccoli florets
50 gr melted ghee butter
1 cup grated cheese
Salt and spices to taste

Servings 4 pieces

Fat 44
Protein 16,6
Carbs 6,8
Fiber 2,4
Calories 484

Instructions

- Preheat the oven to 425F
- Bring the water to boil and put the broccoli florets in it, remove from the heat and leave for about 15 min
- Remove the water and put broccoli into the baking form
- Add melted ghee butter, salt and spices
- Put grated cheese on the top evenly
- Bake in the oven until cheese on the top is slightly browned

Brussels Sprouts With Bacon

Prep time 7 min
Cook time 20 min

Ingredients

1½ pounds trimmed Brussels sprouts
2 tablespoons ghee butter
1 cup chopped kale
3 boiled eggs
1 cup chopped shallot
2 strips diced bacon
Salt and pepper to taste
2 tablespoons chopped almonds

Servings 4 pieces

Fat 15,1
Protein 14,8
Carbs 25
Fiber 7
Calories 273

Instructions

- Bring water to a boil
- Add the Brussels sprouts and kale and keep in the water for 1 minute
- Remove the vegetables from the water and rinse with cold water, dry with a paper towel
- Place the bacon in a skillet over medium heat, cook for 5 minutes until browned
- Remove the bacon to a plate and set aside, let the fat dry
- Add the butter and shallot to the skillet and sauté for 2 minutes
- Add the Brussels sprouts, kale and chopped nuts, season with salt and pepper and mix well
- Sauté for 7-10 minutes
- Cut the boiled eggs in halves
- Transfer vegetables to the plate, top with the bacon and boiled eggs.

73

Zucchini and Tomato Gratin

<table>
<tr>
<td>

Prep time: 10 min
Cook time: 18 min

</td>
<td>

Ingredients

1 zucchini
2 strips diced bacon
1 cup chopped onions
½ cup grated Parmesan cheese
Himalayan rock salt to taste
Pepper to taste
6 cherry tomatoes
½ cup chopped greens

</td>
</tr>
<tr>
<td>

Servings 4 pieces

Fat 6
Protein 7,4
Carbs 12
Fiber 3,6
Calories 122

</td>
<td>

Instructions

- Preheat the oven to 425°F
- Put the diced bacon and chopped onions in a cast-iron skillet over medium heat
- Sauté for about 5-6 minutes until the bacon is cooked through
- Meanwhile, cut the zucchini into thin rounds and cherry tomatoes in halves
- Place zucchini over the onions and bacon in the skillet
- Add half of the Parmesan cheese and half of the chopped greens
- Add another layer of zucchini and top with the remaining Parmesan, greens and the tomatoes
- Place the skillet to the oven and bake for about 10-12 minutes
- Serve hot with a green salad

</td>
</tr>
</table>

Cauliflower Risotto with Parmesan

Prep time: 5 min
Cook time: 25 min

Servings 4 pieces

Fat 7,9
Protein 7,4
Carbs 7,2
Fiber 3,5
Calories 126

Ingredients

450 gr cauliflower florets
100 gr champignons
½ cup grated Parmesan cheese
1 cup chicken broth (cooked or store bought)
50 gr heavy cream
1 tablespoon coconut oil
2 garlic cloves
1 teaspoon oregano
½ teaspoon paprika
Himalayan rock salt to taste

Instructions

- Chop cauliflower florets in the blender
- Cut champignons in small cubes, chop garlic cloves
- Put champignons and garlic cloves in the skillet over medium heat, sauté for 5 minutes until the garlic is fragrant
- Stir in chicken broth and chopped cauliflower. Mix well
- Sauté in the covered pan for about 5 min, then remove the cover and sauté for 10 more minutes
- Add heavy cream, parmesan cheese, and spices. Stir well

Keto Mash

Prep time: 7 min
Cook time: 25 min

Ingredients

500 gr cauliflower florets
2 small onions
2 tablespoons ghee butter
2 tablespoons coconut oil
30 gr pumpkin
½ cup grated parmesan
Salt and pepper to taste
¼ teaspoon garlic powder

Servings 4 pieces

Fat 13,5
Protein 6,8
Carbs 15
Fiber 4,3
Calories 201

Instructions

- Preheat the oven to 425F
- Put cauliflower into the water and boil for 15 minutes
- Meanwhile, chop the onions and pumpkin into small cubes
- Put the onions and pumpkin in the skillet with ghee butter over medium heat, sauté for 5-7 minutes until softened
- Remove the cauliflower from the water, put into the blender and whisk until mashed
- Stir in onions, pumpkin, parmesan, and coconut oil, mix well and blend until even and creamy

Quick Keto Pizza

Prep time: 5 min
Cook time: 12 min

Yield 1 serving

Fat 33,7
Protein 26,5
Carbs 37
Fiber 29,6
Calories 509

Ingredients

½ cup mozzarella cheese
2 large eggs
3 tablespoons grated Parmesan cheese
Himalayan rock salt and pepper to taste
1 teaspoon dried oregano
2 tablespoons ghee butter
3 tablespoon tomato sauce
1 tablespoon chopped parsley
1 tablespoon psyllium

Instructions

- Preheat the oven to 420F
- Mix psyllium, salt, and spices in a mixing bowl
- Add eggs and mix with a blender for about 1 minute
- Heat the butter in the skillet over medium heat, spread the mixture inside
- Fry for 2-3 minutes per side or till ready
- Put the tomato sauce on the dough, sprinkle with cheese and put into the oven
- Once the cheese is melted remove pizza from the heat and top with the parsley

Zucchini Stuffed with Chicken

Prep time: 8 min
Cook time: 30 min

Yield 2 serving

Fat 52,3
Protein 63,9
Carbs 12
Fiber 4,3
Calories 746

Ingredients

2 large zucchinis
100 gr broccoli florets
200 gr grilled chicken (home-made or store-bought)
2 tablespoons heavy cream
2 tablespoons coconut oil
1 cup cheddar cheese
Chopped dill to taste
Salt and pepper to taste

Instructions

- Preheat the oven to 425F
- Cut the zucchini in halves lengthwise
- Remove the pulp with a big spoon leaving the pulp ½ inch thick
- Add coconut oil in each half, season with salt and pepper
- Put in the baking form and place in the oven for about 10 min
- Meanwhile, shred the chicken and chop broccoli florets, grate cheddar cheese
- Mix chicken, broccoli and heavy cream in a bowl
- Remove zucchini from the oven and fill with the mixture
- Top with grated cheddar cheese and dill, place in the oven for 10-15 minutes
- Serve with heavy cream or keto mayo

Keto Caprese

Prep time: 5 min
Cook time: 25 min

Ingredients

1 tablespoon olive oil
150 gr tomatoes
100 gr mozzarella cheese
1 tablespoon chopped cilantro
1 tablespoon lemon juice
Salt and pepper to taste

Yield 2 serving

Fat 18,4
Protein 11,8
Carbs 4,2
Fiber 0,9
Calories 225

Instructions

- Preheat the oven to 400F
- Cut the tomatoes in 2 halves, place in the baking dish
- Season with salt and pepper, top with the chopped cilantro
- Cook for 20 minutes
- Meanwhile, slice mozzarella cheese
- Top the half of tomatoes with the mozzarella and top with the other halves
- Bake for 5 more minutes
- Sprinkle with the lemon juice

Zucchini Lasagna

Prep time: 10 min
Cook time: 10 min

Ingredients

100 gr zucchini
60 gr ricotta cheese
30 gr mozzarella cheese
3 tablespoons tomato sauce
1 tablespoon coconut oil
1 tablespoon chopped parsley

Yield 1 serving

Fat 28,2
Protein 16,5
Carbs 8,3
Fiber 1,9
Calories 340

Instructions

- Preheat the oven to 380F
- Cut the zucchini into thin slices
- Brush the bottom of the baking form with coconut oil, place a layer of tomato sauce
- Add a layer of zucchini
- Cover with the layer of ricotta
- Put one more layer of tomato sauce
- Then the layers of zucchini, ricotta and the last tablespoon of tomato sauce
- Top with the layer of mozzarella cheese and sprinkle with the greens
- Bake for 10 minutes

Basil & Mozzarella Pie

Prep time: 7 min
Cook time: 28 min

Ingredients

1 large egg
½ cup shredded parmesan
4 cherry tomatoes
½ cup mozzarella
2 tablespoons chopped fresh basil
2 tablespoons marinade from mozzarella cheese
90 gr almond flour
Salt and pepper to taste

Yield 3 serving

Fat 14,4
Protein 15,6
Carbs 9
Fiber 2,9
Calories 218

Instructions

- Preheat the oven to 380F, prepare a baking sheet
- In a bowl mix the almond flour and mozzarella marinade
- Add parmesan and beat the egg, mix till even
- Make a big ball of this dough and place in the baking sheet
- Press the ball in the middle until it becomes flat, about 0,5 inch thick
- Place the mozzarella slices, basil and cherry tomatoes in the middle of the dough
- Form a pie, leaving the middle of it open
- Bake for 20-25 min

PORK & LAMB

Juicy Pork Medallions

Prep time 8 min
Cook time 15 min

Ingredients

2 lbs pork tenderloins (cut into ½ inch rounds)
2 tablespoons ghee butter
½ cup chopped shallots
3 tablespoons drained capers
4 tablespoons heavy cream
1/2 cup bone broth
Himalayan rock salt and pepper to taste

Yield 4 servings

Fat 29
Protein 69,8
Carbs 4,1
Fiber 0,2
Calories 573

Instructions

- Flatten pork rounds to ½ inch thickness
- Add salt and pepper to taste
- Preheat ghee butter in the cast-iron skillet and sauté tenderloin rounds for 5 minutes each side
- Remove the pork from the skillet and put in the plate
- Put shallots in the skillet and sauté for 1 minute
- Add sauce and heavy cream and boil until sauce is thick enough to coat a spoon
- Mix in capers and return tenderloins to sauce in skillet to cook through

Pork chops

Prep time 10 min **Cook time 20 min**	*Ingredients* 1-kilo pork fillet 4 chicken eggs Red pepper to taste Salt to taste 2 teaspoon heavy cream

Yield 8 servings

Fat 12,7
Protein 34,4
Carbs 1,5
Fiber 0
Calories 261

Instructions

- Rinse pork meat and dry with a paper towel
- Cut pork in thin slices
- With a sharp knife make small notches far and wide on the pork slices
- Season with salt and pepper
- In the bowl mix eggs, heavy cream and salt. Whip well
- Put pork chops into this mix one by one
- Heat the pan with ghee oil and fry pork chops 5 minutes per side or until browned
- Put chops on the paper towel to remove excess fat

Roasted Pork with Cauliflower

Prep time 10 min
Cook time 20 min

Ingredients

1 ½ pound of boneless pork tenderloin
2 cups cauliflower florets
1 tablespoon coconut oil
1 teaspoon oregano
Himalayan rock salt to taste
2 tablespoons olive oil

Yield 4 servings

Fat 15
Protein 34
Carbs 2,9
Fiber 1,4
Calories 275

Instructions

- In a glass mix olive oil, oregano, salt and pepper
- Season the pork with this mix
- Heat the coconut oil in a large skillet over medium-high heat
- Add the pork and cook for 2 to 3 minutes on each side until browned
- Put the cauliflower in the skillet around the pork
- Reduce the heat to low, then cover the skillet and cook for 10 minutes
- Slice the pork and serve with the cauliflower and green salad

Pork with Bacon and Cauliflower

Prep time 10 min
Cook time 25 min

Ingredients

1 ¼ pounds boneless pork tenderloin
8 slices fresh bacon
1 tablespoon coconut oil
Salt and pepper to taste
2 cups cauliflower florets

Yield 4 servings

Fat 23,1
Protein 43,8
Carbs 4,4
Fiber 1,3
Calories 397

Instructions

- Preheat the oven to 400°F and season the pork with salt and pepper.
- Wrap the pork in bacon and place on a foil-lined roasting pan
- Roast for 25 minutes
- Meanwhile, preheat the coconut oil in a skillet over medium heat
- Add the cauliflower and sauté for 10 minutes until it becomes crispy
- Turn on the broiler and place the pork under it to crisp the bacon
- Slice the pork and serve with the cauliflower

Lamb Chops with Zucchini

Prep time 7 min
Cook time 20 min

Ingredients

8 bone-in lamb chops
Salt and pepper to taste
1 tablespoon fresh chopped rosemary
1 tablespoon coconut oil
1 tablespoon ghee butter
1 zucchini

Yield 4 servings

Fat 15,1
Protein 35,1
Carbs 2,2
Fiber 0,9
Calories 287

Instructions

- Season the lamb with salt and pepper and add rosemary
- Heat the oil in a large skillet over medium-high heat
- Add the lamb chops and cook for 5-7 minutes per side until seared
- Meanwhile, cut zucchini in small cubes
- Remove the lamb chops from the skillet and set aside on the plate
- Put the zucchini in the skillet, fry them for 10 minutes
- Serve the lamb with the zucchini

Creamy Pork with Mushrooms

Prep time 7 min
Cook time 30 min

Yield 3 servings

Fat 21,1
Protein 31,6
Carbs 12
Fiber 3,5
Calories 362

Ingredients

300 gr pork sirloin
8 champignons
1 medium onion
2 garlic cloves
2 tablespoons heavy cream
1 tablespoon cream cheese, softened
1 tablespoon almond flour
½ teaspoon coriander
Salt and pepper to taste
1 tablespoon chopped fresh parsley

Instructions

- Cut the pork into small cubes
- Chop champignons, onion and mince garlic
- Heat the cast-iron skillet and add pork, cook till browned
- Stir in the mushrooms, onion and garlic, salt and spices
- Cook for about 10 minutes, stirring constantly
- Stir in ½ cup water, then cream cheese and almond flour, mix till the sauce is even
- Cook till the sauce thickens for 7-8 minutes
- Top with greens

Tender Fried Pork with Veggies

Prep time 10 min
Cook time 15 min

Ingredients

300 gr pork sirloin
1 red bell pepper
1 medium onion
1 marinated cucumber
1 tablespoon almond flour
½ cup tomato sauce
2 stalks fresh parsley
1 tablespoon ghee oil
Himalayan rock salt and pepper to taste

Yield 2 servings

Fat 17
Protein 26,1
Carbs 15
Fiber 4
Calories 316

Instructions

- Cut the pork into small thin slices
- Heat the cast-iron skillet with ghee oil over medium-high heat, add pork and cook until golden crispy
- While cooking, shred the vegetables, chop the parsley
- Add them to the skillet and cook over high heat for about 4-6 minutes, stirring constantly
- Season with salt and pepper, add tomato sauce
- Reduce the heat and cook for 5-6 minutes or until ready
- Serve with sliced cucumber and chopped greens

Creamy Cheese and Bacon Casserole

Prep time 13 min
Cook time 25 min

Yield 4 servings

Fat 44,5
Protein 15,4
Carbs 3,8
Fiber 0,4
Calories 476

Ingredients

150 gr bacon, uncooked
100 gr cream cheese
100 gr heavy cream
150 gr grated cheddar cheese
½ cup keto mayo
1 tomato
5 stalks green onion
2 tablespoons ghee butter

Instructions

- Preheat the oven to 400F
- Heat the ghee butter in the skillet over medium heat
- Slice the bacon and fry it in the skillet for 3-5 minutes, then transfer to a paper towel to remove the fat
- In a small bowl mix keto mayo, heavy cream and cream cheese
- Add the bacon to this mixture and half of cheddar cheese
- Cut the tomato into cubes and add to the bowl, toss well
- Put this mixture into a baking form and cook in the oven for about 15 minutes

FISH & SEAFOOD

Lemon Codfish

Prep time 12 min
Cook time 25 min

Ingredients

400 gr codfish fillet
2 tablespoons ghee butter
2 garlic cloves
1 lemon
Salt and spices to taste

Yield 2 servings

Fat 11,6
Protein 30,5
Carbs 3,7
Fiber 0,9
Calories 238

Instructions

- Preheat the oven to 425F
- Remove all bones from the fish and slice the fillet
- Remove the skin from the lemon
- Chop the lemon skin and the garlic cloves
- Mix lemon skin, garlic, salt and spices with melted ghee butter in the bowl
- Cut the lemon into halves, squeeze the juice from one half and cut the other one into thin rounds
- Sprinkle the fish with salt, place in the baking dish and add the lemon-butter mixture
- Bake in the oven for 20 minutes
- Put the sliced lemon on the top and bake for 5 more minutes

Juicy Garlic Shrimps

Prep time 8 min Cook time 22 min	*Ingredients* 1 pound fresh peeled shrimps 2 garlic cloves 2 tablespoons coconut oil 2 tablespoons ghee butter Himalayan rock salt to taste ¼ cup dry white wine 1 tablespoon fresh chopped parsley 1 tablespoon oregano Red and black pepper to taste ½ tablespoon lemon juice
Yield 2 servings	*Instructions* • Heat the ghee oil in a large skillet over medium-high heat • Chop garlic and mix spices with salt in a small bowl • Place the shrimps in the skillet and cook 2-3 minutes
Fat 25,4 Protein 27,6 Carbs 3,4 Fiber 1,1 Calories 365	• Add garlic and cook until garlic is fragrant • Pour in wine and lemon juice and cook for 5 minutes • Add the spice mixture and coconut oil and stir until combined • Continue cooking over medium-low heat for about 5-6 minutes until the sauce thickens • Remove from the heat and keep in a cool place for 2-3 minutes • Serve with greens

Asian Shrimp Salad

Prep time 7 min
Cook time 18 min

Ingredients

1 pound peeled, deveined shrimps
½ cup fresh chopped parsley
2 tablespoons coconut oil
½ tablespoon lemon juice
½ cup full-fat coconut milk
2 small red bell peppers
1 avocado
¼ cup chopped almonds
2 cups chopped greens (spinach, cilantro, etc)
½ teaspoon (or to taste) red pepper flakes

Yield 2 servings

Fat 31,4
Protein 34
Carbs 23
Fiber 11,3
Calories 488

Instructions

- Heat coconut oil in a skillet over medium-high heat
- Put the shrimps to the skillet and cook for about 5 minutes (until pink and curled)
- Remove from the heat and set aside
- Pour remaining oil from the pan into a small bowl
- Add lemon juice, chopped parsley, red pepper flakes, coconut milk, mix well and set aside
- Put greens, bell peppers, and chopped avocado on the large plate
- Top with shrimps and season with coconut milk mixture
- Garnish with chopped almonds

Asian Style Salmon

Prep time 7 min
Cook time 18 min

Ingredients

12 ounces salmon fillet
1 red bell pepper
1 orange bell pepper
Himalayan rock salt to taste
Red and black pepper to taste
1 tablespoon coconut oil

Yield 2 servings

Fat 31,4
Protein 34
Carbs 23
Fiber 11,3
Calories 488

Instructions

- Preheat the oven to 400F and place salmon in the baking form
- Sprinkle with salt, pepper and coconut oil
- Bake 8-10 minutes or until salmon is medium fried
- Meanwhile, preheat coconut oil in the pan over low-medium heat
- Slice bell peppers, add to the skillet and season with salt and spices
- Sauté for about 8 minutes or until browned
- Remove from the heat and spread the mixture over the salmon
- Leave to rest for 2-3 minutes before serving

Rosemary Trout

Prep time 5 min
Cook time 13 min

Yield 6 servings

Fat 21,3
Protein 40,3
Carbs 1,3
Fiber 0,5
Calories 368

Ingredients

2 pounds fresh trout
½ cup ghee butter
Himalayan rock salt to taste
Red pepper to taste
2 tablespoons fresh chopped rosemary
3 tablespoons lime juice

Instructions

- Cut the fish lengthwise and season with salt and pepper
- Preheat the ghee oil in the pan
- Place fish in the pan and fry for 5-6 minutes each side
- Once done, remove the fish and set aside
- Add the lime juice and rosemary to the oil in the pan and cook for 1 minute
- Garnish the trout with this sauce

Juicy Halibut Steak

Prep time 5 min
Cook time 13 min

Yield 1 servings

Fat 24
Protein 31,1
Carbs 5,5
Fiber 3,7
Calories 307

Ingredients

6 ounces fresh halibut steak
1 tablespoon ghee oil
1 tablespoon fresh chopped dill
1 tablespoon lemon juice
½ tablespoon Dijon mustard
1 avocado

Instructions

- Mix the chopped dill, lemon juice and mustard in a small mixing bowl
- Brush both sides of the halibut steak with this mixture
- Heat the ghee oil in the pan
- Put fish in the frying pan and cook for about 7-10 minutes each side
- Serve with sliced avocado

Salmon with Bacon

Prep time 5 min
Cook time 18 min

Yield 1 servings

Fat 34,4
Protein 34,8
Carbs 1
Fiber 0
Calories 467

Ingredients

2 fresh salmon fillets
6 thick slices uncooked bacon
2 tablespoons ghee butter
4 tablespoons sour cream
Garlic powder to taste
Salt and pepper to taste

Instructions

- Heat the ghee oil in the skillet
- Wrap 3 slices of bacon around each salmon fillet, completely covering it
- Place the bacon-wrapped salmon fillets into the skillet and cook for about 6-8 minutes each side or until browned
- Mix the sour cream with the garlic powder, spices and salt in a bowl and serve the salmon with this sauce

Keto Tuna Casserole

Prep time 12 min
Cook time 10 min

Ingredients

1 can of tuna (large)
3 tablespoons keto mayo
3 hard-boiled eggs
2 cups shredded cheddar cheese
1 teaspoon chopped fresh parsley
Himalayan rock salt to taste

Yield 1 servings

Fat 47,5
Protein 77,9
Carbs 3,1
Fiber 0
Calories 560

Instructions

- Preheat the oven to 425F
- Mix keto mayo with the chopped parsley and salt in a mixing bowl
- Add tuna, mix well and place the mixture into the casserole dish
- Add a layer of cheddar cheese
- Slice up eggs and put them on the top of the cheese
- Put a thin layer of keto mayo on the top
- Top with one extra layer of cheese
- Place the dish into the oven and cook for 8-10 minutes until the cheese is crispy

Cheesy Shrimps

Prep time 10 min
Cook time 23 min

Ingredients

1 pound peeled and deveined large shrimps
1 cup ghee butter
1 cup cream cheese
1 cup shredded cheddar cheese
1 cup grated Parmesan cheese
6 champignons
¼ cup diced onions
1 cup bone broth

Yield 4 servings

Fat 46,2
Protein 37
Carbs 3,9
Fiber 0,4
Calories 571

Instructions

- Preheat the broiler to 425F
- Melt ½ cup of ghee in the cast-iron skillet over medium-high heat
- Meanwhile, slice the champignons
- Add the onions and mushrooms to the skillet and sauté for 5-6 minutes, stirring occasionally
- Add the shrimps and sauté for 4 minutes, until the shrimps are cooked through
- Meanwhile, mix the broth and cream cheese in a blender and puree until smooth
- Add this mixture to the skillet
- Add the cheddar cheese, place the mixture into a 9-inch square casserole dish and bake in the oven for 8-10 minutes

Juicy Salmon with Brussels Sprouts

Prep time 10 min
Cook time 20 min

Ingredients

500 gr salmon fillet
6 tablespoons pesto sauce
1 cup shredded mozzarella
500 gr Brussels sprouts
5 thin bacon slices
1 tablespoon ghee butter
Salt and pepper to taste

Yield 2 servings

Fat 63,2
Protein 71,3
Carbs 27
Fiber 10,9
Calories 840

Instructions

- Preheat the oven to 420F
- Put the salmon into the baking dish, add salt and pepper
- Brush the fish with the pesto sauce
- Put in the oven and bake for about 15 minutes
- Meanwhile, cut the Brussels sprouts into halves and slice up the bacon into small pieces
- Place the bacon in the skillet with heated ghee oil and add Brussels sprouts
- Reduce the heat twice and cover the skillet with the cap. Cook for 10 minutes
- 2 minutes before done add some water in the skillet to soften the bacon
- Garnish the salmon with Brussels sprouts

Fried Mackerel with Tomatoes

<table>
<tr><td>

Prep time 7 min
Cook time 15 min

</td><td>

Ingredients

4 gutted mackerels
Black pepper to taste
Himalayan rock salt to taste
1 teaspoon coriander powder
3 tablespoons olive oil
2 tablespoons chopped rosemary
2 garlic cloves
800 gr tomatoes
1 fresh red chili pepper
2 tablespoons heavy cream
2 tablespoons chopped basil

</td></tr>
<tr><td>

Yield 4 servings

Fat 31,3
Protein 22,9
Carbs 9,7
Fiber 3,2
Calories 399

</td><td>

Instructions

- Make 2 transversal cuts on the mackerels (both sides), leaving approximately 0,8 inch to the bones
- Brush the fish with salt, pepper, and coriander
- Put the fish into the cast-iron skillet with preheated olive oil
- Season with rosemary and chopped garlic
- Cook 5-6 minutes per side till crispy
- Meanwhile, cut the tomatoes and place to the large platter
- Put chopped chili pepper on the top
- Place fried mackerel on the top of the salad and garnish with basil leaves

</td></tr>
</table>

Coconut Shrimps with Vitamin Salad

Prep time 18 min
Cook time 12 min

Yield 6 servings

Fat 39,8
Protein 39,2
Carbs 14
Fiber 10,8
Calories 569

Ingredients

1 ½ pound of large shrimp, peeled and deveined
1 ½ cups shredded unsweetened coconut
2 tablespoons coconut oil
1 teaspoon lemon juice
2 eggs
Salt and pepper to taste
½ cup of canned coconut milk
500 gr tomatoes
2 avocados

Instructions

- Pour the coconut into a shallow plate
- Beat the eggs with salt and pepper in a mixing bowl
- Dip the shrimp first in the egg, then in the coconut
- Heat the coconut oil in the skillet over medium-high heat
- Add the shrimp and fry for 1 to 2 minutes per side until browned
- Remove the shrimp to a paper towel and set aside
- Slice the tomatoes and avocados, season with salt and pepper and pour on with the lemon sauce
- Serve with the shrimps

Salmon Pies

Prep time 15 min
Cook time 12 min

Ingredients

8 ounces salmon fillet
1 tablespoon ghee butter
2 tablespoons coconut oil
1 egg
1 tablespoon fresh chopped dill
1 cup diced cauliflower florets
Salt and pepper to taste
½ cup almond flour
2 tablespoons minced onion

Yield 2 servings

Yield 2 servings
Fat 31,3
Protein 27,7
Carbs 6,1
Fiber 2,4
Calories 406

Instructions

- Melt the ghee butter in a skillet over medium heat
- Season cauliflower with salt and pepper and cook in the skillet for 5-6 minutes
- Transfer the cauliflower into a bowl and reheat the skillet
- Place the salmon inside and season with salt and pepper
- Cook the salmon for about 7 minutes and remove from the heat
- Mix the cooked cauliflower with the almond flour, egg, minced onion and chopped dill in a mixing bowl
- Shred the salmon and stir in the bowl, mix well
- Shape the mixture into 6 pies and fry in coconut oil until both sides are browned

Oily Codfish

Prep time 3 min
Cook time 10 min

Yield 3 servings

Fat 9,4
Protein 20,2
Carbs 1
Fiber 0,3
Calories 169

Ingredients

400 gr codfish fillet
¼ lemon
½ cup ghee butter
½ teaspoon garlic powder
Salt and pepper to taste
½ teaspoon paprika
½ teaspoon dried basil leaves
1 stalk of dill

Instructions

- Mix all spices in a small mixing bowl
- Slice the fillet, brush each slice with the spice mixture
- Heat 2 tablespoons ghee butter in the skillet over medium-high heat, fry the fish 2-3 minutes one side
- Meanwhile, chop the dill
- Reduce the heat to medium, turn the fillet to other side, add the rest of the oil and top with the chopped dill
- Cook for 3-5 minutes
- Sprinkle with the lemon juice

SALADS

Macadamia Chicken Salad

Prep time 7 min
Cook time 3 min

Ingredients

400 gr cooked chicken breast (grilled or baked)
150 gr green salad
½ cup keto mayo
½ cup macadamia nuts
1 tablespoon cilantro
2 tablespoons basil leaves

Yield 4 servings

Fat 34,8
Protein 70,2
Carbs 7,3
Fiber 3,5
Calories 623

Instructions

- Shred the chicken breast, chop macadamia and all greens
- Mix all ingredients in the bowl
- Season with salt and pepper, add keto mayo

Tuna Healthy Bowl

**Prep time 10 min
Cook time 1 min**

Ingredients

8 ounces tuna fillet
¼ cup chopped cilantro
1 avocado
2 tablespoon coconut oil
½ cup chopped pecan nuts
Salt and pepper to taste
½ red grapefruit
¼ cup grated parmesan

Yield 2 servings

Fat 50,9
Protein 29,2
Carbs 14,6
Fiber 9,4
Calories

Instructions

- Cut tuna fillet into small cubes, season with salt and pepper and place in a bowl
- Slice grapefruit and avocado and add to the bowl
- Mince cilantro, chop pecan nuts and add into the bowl
- Add coconut oil, gently toss until combined
- Add grated parmesan on the top

Macadamia & Tuna Salad

Prep time 10 min
Cook time 1 min

Yield 1 servings

Fat 70,5
Protein 48,7
Carbs 22
Fiber 16,5
Calories 800

Ingredients

1 large can of tuna
1 teaspoon coconut oil
2 tablespoons keto mayo
¼ cup chopped macadamia nuts
1 stalk green onion
1 avocado
Salt and pepper to taste

Instructions

- Open the can and drain tuna
- Put into the mixing bowl
- Add in the keto mayo, coconut oil, salt and pepper. Mix gently
- Slice the green onion and add to the bowl
- Chop the macadamia nuts and add them to the bowl. Mix well
- Slice avocado and top the salad with it

Zucchini Salad with Bacon & Blue Cheese

Prep time 5 min
Cook time 13 min

Ingredients

2 small zucchinis
2 tablespoon coconut oil
1-ounce blue cheese
½ cup spinach
1 cup shredded kale
2 hard-boiled eggs
4 thin slices cooked bacon
Salt and pepper to taste

Yield 1 servings

Instructions

- Remove the skin from zucchini, cut them into cubes
- Heat the coconut oil in the skillet over medium heat, add zucchini
- Cook for 5-6 minutes, stirring occasionally
- Transfer to a bowl
- Shred the eggs and cheese
- Slice the bacon and add to the bowl
- Add all remaining ingredients, season with salt and pepper and toss well

Fat 60,5
Protein 36,5
Carbs 17
Fiber 3,9
Calories 740

Green Salad with Bacon and Sesame Seeds

Prep time 5 min **Cook time 15 min**	*Ingredients* 1 teaspoon coconut oil 1 teaspoon olive oil ½ avocado 1 cup mixed greens (spinach, lettuce, rocket) 1 cup shredded kale 2 eggs 6 slices uncooked bacon 2 tablespoons sesame seeds
Yield 1 servings	*Instructions* • Heat the coconut oil in the sauté pan over medium heat • Add the bacon and cook for 3-4 minutes until browned • Remove from the heat and set aside • Beat the eggs, scramble and add to the skillet • Add kale and cook till it changes the color • Remove from the heat and mix with the bacon in the bowl • Slice avocado, chop greens and also place in the bowl • Mix well, top with sesame seeds and season with olive oil, salt and pepper
Fat 48 **Protein 36,6** **Carbs 29,3** **Fiber 14,8** **Calories 720**	

Salmon and Bell Pepper Salad

Prep time 10 min
Cook time 7 min

Ingredients

2 pre-cooked filet salmon (grilled or fried)
3 cups red kale
2 tablespoons chopped almonds
2 tablespoons olive oil
2 teaspoons lemon zest
1 teaspoon lemon juice
1 green bell pepper
Salt and pepper to taste
14 boiled asparagus spears

Yield 2 servings

Fat 30,1
Protein 46,3
Carbs 17
Fiber 6,2
Calories 512

Instructions

- Chop the bell pepper and kale, cut asparagus and put into the bowl
- In a bowl mix olive oil, lemon zest, lemon juice, almonds, salt and pepper
- Add the mixture to the bowl, toss well
- Slice the salmon and place on the top of the salad

Goat Cheese Salad

Prep time 10 min
Cook time 15 min

Yield 4 servings

Fat 38,3
Protein 18
Carbs 4,4
Fiber 2,5
Calories 434

Ingredients

½ pound diced uncooked bacon
8-ounces goat cheese log
2 cups basil leaves
1 cup chopped parsley
½ avocado
4 tablespoons red wine vinegar
3 tablespoons avocado oil
1 teaspoon mustard
Salt to taste
1 teaspoon black pepper

Instructions

- Heat the oil in a skillet over medium heat
- Sauté the diced bacon in a skillet for 5 minutes or until crispy
- Transfer the bacon to a bowl
- Cut the goat cheese log, make 8 medallions about a ¼ inch thick
- Fry the medallions in the hot skillet over medium heat for 1-2 minutes per side or until golden
- Remove the cheese medallions from the skillet and set aside on a plate
- Put the vinegar, oil, mustard, salt, pepper to the skillet and stir well to combine. Stir in the bacon
- Chop the greens and slice the avocado
- Put on a large plate and top with cheese medallions, pour the sauce on the top

Spinach & Blue Cheese Salad

Prep time 8 min
Cook time 10 min

Ingredients

3 cups fresh spinach
1 medium red onion
½ cup blue cheese
3 tablespoons chopped almonds
6 slices uncooked bacon
1 tablespoon avocado oil

Yield 1 servings

Fat 51,4
Protein 40,7
Carbs 12
Fiber 7,2
Calories 695

Instructions

- Heat the skillet over medium heat and cook the bacon 2-3 minutes each side
- Transfer to a plate, let it rest for 2 minutes then chop it
- Cut the onion into thin rings and press a bit with the knife to soften it
- Shred blue cheese
- Place the spinach leaves to the bottom of the salad bowl, cover with the onion rings, shredded cheese and bacon, top with almonds
- Season with oil and pepper

Pecan Cheese Salad

Prep time 5 min
Cook time 10 min

Ingredients

30 gr pecan nuts, chopped
50 gr mozzarella cheese
3 cups fresh spinach or other greens
4 bacon slices
2 tablespoons olive oil
½ cup grated parmesan

Yield 1 servings

Fat 64,6
Protein 22,7
Carbs 8,9
Fiber 5
Calories 630

Instructions

- Heat the oil in the skillet and cook the bacon slices for 2-3 minutes per side until browned
- Transfer to a plate
- Cut spinach leaves and mozzarella cheese (make small cubes)
- Mix all ingredients in a bowl
- Top with nuts, grated parmesan and season with oil and pepper

Quick Shrimp Salad

Prep time 5 min
Cook time 9 min

Yield 2 servings

Fat 15,1
Protein 26,9
Carbs 3,7
Fiber 1,1
Calories 259

Ingredients

8 ounces fresh shrimps
1 tablespoon ghee butter
2 cups fresh spinach
1 tablespoon basil leaves
¼ cup green olives
1 tablespoon olive oil
Cayenne pepper and Himalayan salt to taste

Instructions

- Heat the ghee butter in the skillet and fry shrimps for 7-8 minutes
- Chop the spinach and basil
- In the bowl mix cooked shrimps, greens, olives, season with salt, pepper and olive oil
- Serve cool

Keto Cheese & Veggies Salad

Prep time 5 min
Cook time 5 min

Ingredients

50 gr tomatoes
50 gr cucumbers
50 gr green salad
50 gr cheddar cheese
1 tablespoon olive oil
1 tablespoon chopped dill
½ teaspoon chopped garlic
1 tablespoon Dijon mustard
1 large egg
Salt and pepper to taste

Yield 1 servings

Fat 20,6
Protein 9,4
Carbs 8,8
Fiber 2,3
Calories 244

Instructions

- Mix olive oil, greens and garlic in a bowl
- Cut the veggies, the egg and the cheese into small cubes, combine in a bowl
- Season with Dijon mustard and with spice mixture

Chicken & Lettuce Salad

Prep time 5 min
Cook time 20 min

Yield 4 servings

Fat 30,8
Protein 30,5
Carbs 8,5
Fiber 2,7
Calories 422

Ingredients

450 gr chicken thighs, boneless
5 cherry tomatoes
230 gr uncooked bacon
1 tablespoon ghee butter
250 gr lettuce salad
Himalayan rock salt and pepper to taste
2/3 cup keto mayo
½ teaspoon garlic powder

Instructions

- Slice the bacon
- Heat the butter in the skillet, fry the bacon till golden crispy (4-6 minutes)
- Meanwhile, mince the chicken meat
- Remove from the skillet and reheat the oil
- Place the chicken into the skillet, add salt and pepper, fry for 12-15 minutes
- While frying, cut the cherry tomatoes in halves, cut the salad
- Add chicken and bacon
- Mix the mayo with the garlic powder and season the salad with this mixture

EGGS

Eggs with Tomatoes

Prep time 5 min
Cook time 25 min

Yield 2 servings

Fat 14,5
Protein 14
Carbs 15
Fiber 6,5
Calories 243

Ingredients

4 eggs
1 small onion
1 garlic clove
1 green bell pepper
3 medium tomatoes
¼ tablespoon dried paprika
¼ tablespoon dried oregano
Salt and spices to taste
1 tablespoon ghee butter

Instructions

- Chop the onion and garlic, dice the bell pepper and tomatoes into small slices
- Heat the skillet with ghee butter and saute the onion with garlic for 3-4 minutes
- Then add tomatoes, pepper, salt, paprika, and oregano, saute for 5-7 minutes
- Beat the eggs, reduce the heat and cook in a covered skillet for about 10 minutes
- Top with chopped greens

Keto Scramble

Prep time 5 min
Cook time 28 min

Ingredients

8 ounces chicken sausages (check the labels for gluten-free products)
3 eggs
½ avocado
½ tomato
1 small yellow squash
Salt and spices to taste

Yield 2 servings

Fat 32,5
Protein 44,1
Carbs 9,4
Fiber 4,2
Calories 489

Instructions

- Remove the casing from the sausages, cut them into thin rounds
- Place the sausages to the frying pan and cook over medium heat for 10 minutes
- Meanwhile, dice the squash and tomato
- Transfer sausages to a plate, leave the fat in the pan
- Reduce the heat and saute squash and tomato in the pan for 5-7 minutes
- Beat the eggs to a bowl and whisk well
- Pour in to the skillet with squash and tomatoes, cook for 4-5 minutes
- Season with spices and salt, cook for 2-3 more minutes
- Top the scramble with sliced avocado

Omelet with Bacon and Mushrooms

Prep time 5 min
Cook time 27 min

Ingredients

2 large eggs
6 slices cooked bacon
2 tablespoons grated parmesan
3 tablespoons dried mushrooms
2 tablespoons coconut oil

Yield 1 servings

Fat 67
Protein 43,1
Carbs 3
Fiber 0,1
Calories 779

Instructions

- Dunk dried mushrooms in the boiled water for 7-8 minutes
- Then dice into thin straws
- Cut the bacon into small cubes
- Beat the eggs to a bowl and whisk well
- Heat the frying pan with the oil
- Add the eggs, bacon and diced mushrooms, cook for 10-12 minutes
- Season with salt and pepper and top with the grated cheese

Mozzarella Omelet

Prep time 7 min
Cook time 8 min

Yield 2 servings

Fat 37
Protein 27,5
Carbs 11,9
Fiber 3,9
Calories 483

Ingredients

3 large tomatoes
4 large eggs
2 tablespoons fresh basil
1 red chili pepper
100 gr mozzarella cheese
2 tablespoons olive oil
2 tablespoons red vinegar
Salt and black pepper to taste

Instructions

- Slice the tomatoes into thin rounds
- Season with ½ tablespoon olive oil and red vinegar, salt and pepper
- Chop the basil leaves and mix with salt and olive oil
- Dice the chili pepper and shred mozzarella into small cubes
- Heat the large skillet with olive oil and beat in the eggs, cook till ready, stirring occasionally
- Transfer eggs to a large plate
- Place mozzarella in the middle of the eggs, spray with the mixture of oil and basil, let it rest a bit
- Meanwhile, slice the tomatoes
- Carefully fold the omelet in half, garnish with tomatoes and chili pepper

Frittata with Sausages

Prep time 5 min
Cook time 25 min

Yield 2 servings

Fat 36,4
Protein 23,3
Carbs 22,1
Fiber 6,4
Calories 509

Ingredients

4 eggs
2 chicken sausages (without casing)
8 cherry tomatoes
2 tablespoons fresh parsley
2 tablespoons fresh cilantro
Salt and black pepper to taste
2 tablespoons ghee oil

Instructions

- Preheat the oven to 400F
- Cut the sausages into thin rounds
- Cut cherry tomatoes in halves
- Heat the skillet over medium-high heat and add the sausages, cook for 2-3 minutes per side until light-golden
- Add the tomatoes, toss and cook for 3 minutes
- While cooking mince the cilantro and parsley
- Beat the eggs in a bowl, add salt and pepper and whip slightly
- Stir in the skillet over sausages and tomatoes
- Place the skillet to the preheated oven for 10-12 minutes
- Serve hot

Omelet with Cheese and Avocado

Prep time 2 min
Cook time 7 min

Ingredients

4 eggs
1 avocado
1 cucumber
4 tablespoons cream cheese
1 teaspoon lemon juice
1 tablespoon olive oil
1 tablespoon ghee butter
Salt and pepper to taste

Yield 2 servings

Fat 41,2
Protein 15,3
Carbs 14
Fiber 7
Calories 468

Instructions

- Heat the skillet with ghee butter
- Beat the eggs in the skillet, add salt and slightly mix. Fry for 3-4 minutes
- Slice avocado and cucumber, season with salt, pepper and olive oil, mix well
- Put the fried eggs in the plate, put the layer of cream cheese and top with veggies

Keto Rolls with Sausages

Prep time 5 min
Cook time 30 min

Ingredients

10 eggs
150 gr cheddar cheese
5 bacon slices, cooked
5 chicken sausages, cooked
2 tablespoon ghee butter
Salt and pepper to taste

Yield 5 servings

Fat 31,7
Protein 28,2
Carbs 2,3
Fiber 0
Calories 412

Instructions

- In a bowl mix 2 eggs and put into the skillet with heated ghee butter
- Add salt and pepper, fry for 3 minutes
- Cut the sausages into halves lengthwise and grate the cheese
- Once almost ready, put a layer of parmesan on the top, then a half of the sausage and the bacon slice
- Wrap the omelet and turn around carefully
- Fry for 5 more minutes and remove from the skillet
- Repeat 4 more times

BEEF

Spinach and Meat Casserole

Prep time 5 min
Cook time 35 min

Yield 2 servings

Fat 30,4
Protein 63,3
Carbs 9,9
Fiber 1,5
Calories 569

Ingredients

200 gr fresh spinach
2 small onions
1 garlic clove
½ cup cream
150 gr ounces minced meat, uncooked
100 gr mozzarella
Salt and pepper to taste
1 tablespoon ghee butter

Instructions

- Preheat the oven to 420F
- Chop the onions and garlic
- Heat the ghee butter in the skillet and fry the onion with garlic for 3-4 minutes until softens
- Add minced meat, cook for 5-7 minutes
- Meanwhile, shred mozzarella cheese
- Place the spinach to the bottom of the baking form, cover with the layer of the onion, garlic, and minced meat
- Top with cream, season with salt and spices
- Sprinkle with the half of shredded cheese
- Cook for 20 minutes. Top with the rest of the cheese

Bison Steak with Avocado and Tomato Sauce

Prep time 7 min
Cook time 25 min

Yield 2 servings

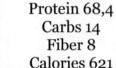

Fat 32,8
Protein 68,4
Carbs 14
Fiber 8
Calories 621

Ingredients

1 pound ground grass-fed bison
1 small yellow squash
2 tablespoons coconut oil
1 diced red pepper
2 cups fresh spinach
1 avocado
Himalayan rock salt and ground pepper to taste

Instructions

- In a sauté pan heat the coconut oil and cook bison for 5-7 minutes until browned
- Meanwhile, cut the squash and mince the spinach
- Add the pepper and squash and sauté for 3-4 minutes
- Add tomato sauce and spinach, season with salt
- Cover the pan and simmer for 15-17 minutes
- Serve with sliced avocado

☐

Beef with Spinach and Parmesan

Prep time 5 min
Cook time 25 min

Ingredients

½ pound ground beef
2 cups fresh spinach
2 tablespoons MCT oil
½ cup grated Parmesan cheese
1 onion
½ teaspoon Himalayan rock salt
½ teaspoon ground black pepper
½ teaspoon cumin powder

Yield 2 servings

Fat 27,4
Protein 45
Carbs 7,8
Fiber 2
Calories 433

Instructions

- Heat the oil in a large cast-iron skillet over medium heat
- Add the onions and cook for 10-15 minutes, until the onions are soft and light brown
- While the onions are frying, dice the spinach, cut the meat into cubes
- Increase the heat to high and add the ground beef to the skillet
- Cook the meat for about 7 minutes, occasionally stirring until browned
- Add the spinach, salt, cumin, and pepper and cook for 2-3 minutes
- Top with grated parmesan cheese

Cheesy Steak

Prep time 7 min
Cook time 20 min

Yield 2 servings

Fat 62,9
Protein 40,4
Carbs 3,2
Fiber 0,5
Calories 730

Ingredients

12-ounces T-bone steak, about ¾ inch thick
½ teaspoon ground black pepper
1 tablespoon MCT oil
1 teaspoon dried oregano
1 ounce crumbled blue cheese
1 cup blue cheese whip
1 cup heavy cream

Instructions

- Preheat the oven to 400°F
- Brush the meat with the salt, pepper, and oregano both sides
- Heat a cast-iron skillet over medium-high heat, heat MCT oil
- Add the steak and cook until ready (your desired doneness)
- Remove from the heat and let the steak rest for 10 minutes
- Meanwhile, make the blue cheese whip: place the cream in a mixer and mix until stiff peaks form
- Stir in the blue cheese and salt until well blended
- Serve each portion of steak with 2 tablespoons of the blue cheese whip

Keto Cutlets

Prep time 7 min
Cook time 10 min

Ingredients

1 pound fresh minced beef
1 onion, diced
2 medium eggs
Spices and salt to taste
4 tablespoons MCT oil (for the meat)
2 tablespoon ghee oil (for frying)
1 teaspoon psyllium

Yield 3 servings

Fat 23,4
Protein 50
Carbs 7,4
Fiber 3,9
Calories 429

Instructions

- Mix minced meat, diced onions, salt and spices in a bowl
- Add MCT oil and mix well
- Add eggs and psyllium and mix again. Make small cutlets of it (about ½ inch thick)
- Heat the ghee oil in a cast-iron skillet over medium-high heat and place the cutlets
- Fry 6-8 minutes per side till ready. Cutlets should be juicy and soft but well-fried
- Serve with greens

Keto Cheeseburger

Ingredients

1 pound minced beef, uncooked
1 tablespoon ghee butter
1 medium onion
2 garlic cloves
1 tablespoon tomato sauce
1 tablespoon Dijon mustard
Salt and spices to taste
4 fresh tomatoes
½ cup shredded cheddar cheese
4 slices fresh cucumber
1 tablespoon sesame seeds

Prep time 2 min
Cook time 17 min

Yield 2 servings

Fat 32,3
Protein 83
Carbs 29
Fiber 8,1
Calories 774

Instructions

- Heat the cast-iron skillet over medium heat with the ghee butter
- Dice the onion and fry it until soft and light-golden
- Chop the garlic cloves, mix with minced beef in a bowl
- Add this mixture to the skillet and brown it for 6-7 minutes, then let in rest for 5 minutes
- Add tomato sauce, mustard, season with salt and pepper, mix well
- Put the tomatoes ass down. Divide each into six wedges without cutting the fruit completely
- Smooth the slices carefully and fill the core with the meat mixture
- Top with the cucumber slices, grated cheddar, and sesame seeds

Broccoli & Beef

Prep time 20 min
Cook time 15 min

Yield 4 servings

Fat 24,1
Protein 39,7
Carbs 8,9
Fiber 3,7
Calories 412

Ingredients

1 pound beef sirloin
¼ cup tomato sauce
2 cups broccoli florets
3 tablespoons coconut oil
1 teaspoon garlic powder
2 tablespoons almond flour
3 garlic cloves garlic

Instructions

- In a small bowl mix 2 tablespoons of coconut oil, garlic powder, tomato sauce
- Mince garlic and chop broccoli florets
- Cut the beef into small cubes and mix with almond flour
- Add sauce, toss and set aside
- Heat the oil in a large skillet over medium-high heat
- Add the meat with sauce and cook until the meat is brown (6-7 minutes)
- Add broccoli and garlic and fry until broccoli is tender crispy

Made in the USA
Middletown, DE
18 September 2019